Read-About® Geography

Gulf of Mexico

By Pam Zollman

Subject Consultant
John W. Tunnell Jr., PhD
Associate Director and Research Scientist
Harte Research Institute for Gulf of Mexico Studies
Texas A&M University–Corpus Christi
Corpus Christi, Texas

Reading Consultant
Cecilia Minden-Cupp, PhD
Former Director of the Language and Literacy Program
Harvard Graduate School of Education
Cambridge, Massachusetts

Children's Press®
A Division of Scholastic Inc.
New York   Toronto   London   Auckland   Sydney
Mexico City   New Delhi   Hong Kong
Danbury, Connecticut

Designer: Herman Adler Design
Photo Researcher: Caroline Anderson
The photo on the cover shows a pier stretching out into the Gulf of Mexico.

Library of Congress Cataloging-in-Publication Data

Zollman, Pam.
  The Gulf of Mexico / by Pam Zollman.
     p. cm. — (Rookie read-about geography)
  Includes index.
  ISBN 0-516-25035-3 (lib. bdg.)   0-516-29711-2 (pbk.)
  1. Mexico, Gulf of—Juvenile literature. I. Title. II. Series.
  F296.Z65 2006
  916.3'64—dc22   2005026247

JE
ZOL
C.1

7/06

CHILDREN'S PRESS, and ROOKIE READ-ABOUT®,
and associated logos are trademarks and/or registered trademarks
of Scholastic Library Publishing. SCHOLASTIC and associated logos
are trademarks and/or registered trademarks of Scholastic Inc.

1 2 3 4 5 6 7 8 9 10 R 15 14 13 12 11 10 09 08 07 06

No one knows for certain how the Gulf of Mexico formed. It's a mystery!

Some scientists think
it used to be dry land.
Then the land slowly sank.
It formed a huge basin,
or bowl.

Water filled the Gulf
basin. The water in the
Gulf of Mexico is warm
and salty.

UNITED STATES

Houston, Texas •

New Orleans,
Louisiana •

Mobile, Alabama
•

The Gulf Coast

• Tampa,
Florida

Gulf of Mexico

CUBA

• Tampico

Caribbean Sea

• Veracruz

MEXICO

North

West ✦ East

South

SCALE 1 inch = 110 miles

0   Miles   110

0   Kilometers   180

6

The Gulf of Mexico
is almost completely
surrounded by land.
The United States,
Mexico, and Cuba
touch the Gulf.

Seawater flows into the Gulf of Mexico from the Caribbean Sea. This sea lies to the east of Mexico and to the south of Cuba.

This flowing water loops around the eastern part of the Gulf basin. It leaves the Gulf of Mexico and flows into the Atlantic Ocean.

The Caribbean Sea off of Cancún, Mexico

Sandy beaches cover most of the Gulf Coast. Seagulls, sand crabs, and clams live along these beaches.

The Gulf Coast has many mangrove forests and salt marshes. Mangroves are trees that can grow in saltwater. Crocodiles and manatees live in mangrove forests.

Salt marshes are grassy.
Fiddler crabs, snails, and
birds live there.

A Florida lighthouse built near a coral reef in the Gulf of Mexico

Reefs and sandbars exist underwater in the Gulf of Mexico. Reefs are ridges made of coral, oysters, or rock.

Sandbars are raised areas in shallow water. They are made of sand.

Reefs and sandbars are dangerous for boats. The water around sandbars is often shallow. Boats can be damaged if they hit the hard reefs.

But boats can also be harmful to reefs and sandbars. Boats scrape and tear up these areas.

17

Dolphins live in the Gulf
of Mexico.

So do sharks and jellyfish.

Fishing is an important business in the Gulf of Mexico. People catch crabs, oysters, and shrimp. They also catch redfish, flounder, and red snapper.

Much of the United States' gas and oil comes from the Gulf of Mexico. People use machines to pump gas and oil from the Gulf floor.

A platform used for drilling oil in the Gulf of Mexico

Houston, Texas

Veracruz, Mexico

Ships travel through the Gulf of Mexico to the United States and Mexico.

Houston, Texas; New Orleans, Louisiana; Mobile, Alabama; and Tampa, Florida, are port cities in the United States.

Two of Mexico's port cities are Tampico and Veracruz.

Hurricanes sometimes form in the Gulf of Mexico. These storms bring fierce wind and rain. They can cause great damage, like Katrina did in 2005.

Florida palm trees blowing in the fierce winds of
a hurricane

People collecting shells along the Gulf Coast

Winters are warm along the Gulf Coast. People like to fish and collect seashells.

Gulf Coast summers
are hot. People enjoy
swimming, surfing, sailing,
and waterskiing.

What would you like to
do in the Gulf of Mexico?

Words You Know

Caribbean Sea

crocodiles

dolphins

hurricanes

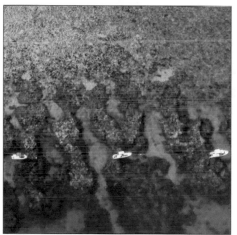

reefs

surfing

31

Index

About the Author

Pam Zollman is the award-winning author of short stories and books for kids. She grew up on the Gulf Coast and loves its warm water. She now lives in the Pocono Mountains of Pennsylvania. Pam dedicates this book to her sister, Colleen Wright, who also loves the Gulf of Mexico.

Photo Credits

Photographs © 2006: Alamy Images: 17 (Dennis Hallinan), 27, 29, 31 bottom right (PhotoStockFile); Corbis Images: 5 (Richard Berenholtz), 3 (Franz Marc Frei), 13 (Raymond Gehman), 21 (Philip Gould), 26 (John Henley), 14, 31 bottom left (Bob Krist), 12, 30 bottom (George McCarthy), 10 (Carl & Ann Purcell), 25, 31 top right (Jim Reed/Jim Reed Photography), 9, 30 top (Royalty-Free); D. Donne Bryant Stock Photography/Chris Sharp: 22 bottom; Getty Images/Hisham F. Ibrahim/Photodisc Red: cover; Nature Picture Library Ltd./Todd Pusser: 18, 31 top left; Seapics.com/Doug Perrine: 19; Superstock, Inc.: 22 top.

Map by Bob Italiano